CHAIN BREAKERS
DO YOU REALLY WANT TO BE FREE?
BY MINISTER MIKE L. W.

Warning!!! This book is only an aide or guide it also contains very serious topical subject matter if you have serious problems or issues by all means seek Professional Godly help, counsel, and advice.

Table of Contents

Introduction   3

A need for Healing   4

You brought it on yourself   7

Are you a good test taker?   10

Getting past your past   15

The path to personal freedom   24

Showing others the path to freedom 28

When the binds are too tight   32

Freedom to serve   41

Choose Life   42

Introduction

Life can be very cruel and unkind. It can even appear to be unfair at times. There are often situations in life where we feel trapped. Closed in or even bound. These situations may last for days, weeks, months, even years. When we converse with people we often tell them how we wish for better days or brighter times. However when it gets down to it in some cases we've been down so long that we've grown accustomed to it. Misery has, over a period of time sadly become acceptable company. So what do we do? How do we break free? How do we break the chains?

It is our goal to help you to do all of the above. To finally break free!!! The fact that you have taken the time to read this is definitely a step in the right direction. We do not nor do we want in any shape form or fashion to appear that we have all of the answers. Because we don't, our goal is to educate and help motivate you to find what will work for you and eventually set you free. Throughout the process we will definitely point you to the one who does have all of the answers. In fact he is the answer!!! However it is up to you whether are not you are willing to take the necessary steps to your personal path to freedom.

A need for healing

(Mat 9:11) And when the Pharisees saw, they said to His disciples, Why does your master eat with tax-collectors and sinners?
(Mat 9:12) But when Jesus heard, He said to them, The ones who are whole do not need a physician, but the ones who are sick. When things are going well in life often we pay little attention to the spiritual aspect of our lives. Things are going fine and God is there when we need him, but the best place for God is to stay where he's at while we enjoy life. Then trouble hits whether of our own doing or from situations and circumstances beyond our control. No matter where it comes from when it hits trouble has a way of getting our attention and keeping it.

In our text we find the Pharisees who sad to say also represent some of those who call themselves Christians today. The Pharisees are commenting on how Jesus would break bread with those that were looked down upon during his time. His response sends a message loud and clear to the church of his day as well as ours. He responded that " *The ones who are whole do not need a physician, but the ones who are sick".* If you are sick and in need of healing God wants to see you healed. As believers those who are in need should be able to turn to us. We should be the vehicle that God uses to bring about healing. The church should never fail to aide those that suffer be it from physical sickness, the cares of life, or the results of someone's personal sin. Those that are hurting should always be able to turn to the church. However today just as in our text that is not always the case. Some churches often resemble the Pharisees by looking down on those that God wants them to help.

So where should you go if you have tried everything and everybody, still you are in trouble. The answer today is the same as back then that answer is Jesus. People can and often do fail but Jesus never fails. At the same time if you are indeed in trouble with nowhere to turn. If there are things in this life that have you bound and you just want to be free Jesus is the answer. Jesus does however use people to help bring about his purpose in our lives.

Everybody is not bad there are still many Godly people all around the world. Sometimes we just tend to be around the wrong folks in or out of church. Then another thing to remember is that people aren't perfect. Yet God still uses people. He'll either send you to someone or send someone to you. It does not have to be in person. It could be in a book such as this, a Bible story, TV, radio, the Internet.

If you have a need for healing then God wants to heal you. Your need may not be one for physical healing, it could be mental, emotional, financial, or situational. Everything may be fine in every aspect of your life however you feel tied down or bound by one area. It could be stifling to the point that emotionally even physically you can't breathe. There is help and hope because God has a way out for you and he will give you the strength to cope.

You must believe and trust God. Regardless of whether you brought your current situation on yourself via bad decisions, sin, and disobedience, whatever the case may be. God loves you he does not love our sin but he does love us and he is always willing to forgive and restore. However the process of forgiveness and restoration does not free us from the consequences of sin or bad decisions.

Yes God is a loving and forgiving God but when we sin there are consequences for our sins. We can't tell God how he should chasten us or how long. God is God and he provided us with a conscience, the Holy Spirit, and his Holy Word, all to guide us through life *(Romans 6:23) For the wages of sin is death, but the gift of God is eternal life through Jesus Christ our Lord.*

When we sin death can be the immediate or future result of those sins. Everyone is scheduled to die except those who will be carried away in the rapture. However we can hasten that appointment by living a lifestyle of sin. Sin is binding whether we realize it or not. It may appear to be fun or attractive but it is deadly. It is only because of grace that God does not immediately take us out of this life when we are living a sinful lifestyle. When in the midst of our sin, it is only through the aide of the Holy Spirit we recognize who God. It is then that we can gain true freedom from the bondage of sin.

You brought it on yourself:

(2Ch 33:10) And Jehovah spoke to Manasseh and to His people, but they would not listen.
(2Ch 33:11) And Jehovah brought on them the commanders of the army of the king of Assyria, who took Manasseh among the thorns and bound him with chains and carried him to Babylon.

In our text we find that the children of Israel had not listened to the voice of God. Led by their king Manasseh they had out sinned nations that the Lord previously destroyed. Manasseh had a laundry list of things he did wrong. He practiced soothsaying, used witchcraft and sorcery, and consulted with mediums and spiritualists. The scripture said that he did much evil in the sight of the Lord. He also practiced Idolatry to the extent that he even put a carved image in the house of God.

In 2nd Chronicles 33:10 God has spoken to Manasseh and the children of Israel but they just would not listen. So in the next verse Manasseh is literally carried off in chains to Babylon. For us Babylon represents the world. When we fail to listen to God through his Holy word and the Holy Spirit then we can find ourselves just as Manasseh did bound. Our bondage can be a result of sin, bad choices, bad company, bad environment, or bad advice.

Whatever the case when it leads us to disobeying God, then Babylon may be, the next stop of our journey through life. When we are in harmony with the world, then we are at odds with God. The scripture even says we become an enemy of God.
(James 4:4) Adulterers and adulteresses! Do you not know that the friendship of the world is enmity *with* God? Therefore whoever desires to be a friend of the world is the enemy of God.

When you decide to follow the crowd and go with the flow of this world then you become an enemy of God. That is definitely not a spot that you want to be in. Don't get me wrong God still loves you and cares for you. God loves the worst sinner that you could think of or find. Once you fall into sin it is you that have decided to become an enemy of God. He is not against you, you are now against him. Once you realize what you have done then what.

(2Chronciles 33:12) And when he was in affliction, he sought Jehovah his God, and humbled himself greatly before the God of his fathers.
(2Chronicles 33:13) And he prayed to Him, and He was entreated of him, and heard his prayer, and brought him again to Jerusalem into his kingdom. And Manasseh knew that Jehovah *is* God.

From this text we see that once Manasseh is literally taken away to Babylon in chains he then seeks out God. Here is someone who rewrote the book on being evil and doing everything that God didn't want him to do. God speaks to him, he doesn't listen. Yet once he loses his freedom and is taken from his home even to another country. Then he humbles himself to the point that he gets God's attention.

8

The verse said that he *humbled himself greatly before the God of his fathers.* Here in lies the key because it is after this act of awesome humility equal to the level of his disobedience. He gets God's attention through humility then God sends him back home. Then as the scripture says *Manasseh knew that Jehovah is God.* Once Manasseh recognized who he was dealing with then he gets his act together. You may have really messed up bringing bondage on yourself. Your solution is the same as Manasseh. You have to go after God in a spirit of repentance and humility. You need to be passionate and intense you should look back in disgust at your sins and mistakes. Then seek God with all that is within you in order that he restores you.

(Joel 2:25) And I will restore to you the years which the swarming locust has eaten, the locust larvae, and the stripping locust, and the cutting locust, My great army which I sent among you.

This verse is often quoted by teachers and preachers. One thing that is often left out is that God lets us know that he was the one who had sent the destruction. After God has chastened us and we have repented then God restores. God loves us and does not want us to lack anything. When you have messed up big time God is waiting to fix up what you messed up. You must make that first step, you must humble self and pray with a heart of true repentance.

Are you a good test taker?

(Job 23:10) But He knows the way that I take; *when* He has tried me, I shall come forth as gold.

(Revelation 2:10) Do not at all fear what you are about to suffer. Behold, the Devil will cast *some* of you into prison, so that you may be tried. And you will have tribulation ten days. Be faithful to death, and I will give you the crown of life.

(Revelation 2:13) I know your works, and where you live, *even* where Satan's seat *is* . And you hold fast My name and have not denied My faith, even in those days in which Antipas *was* My faithful martyr, who was slain among you, where Satan dwells.

Sometimes you're in a situation where it really is not your fault. You have done everything that you felt was right. You live a life that is pleasing in the sight of God. Yet you find yourself in a place of bondage. Somehow or another you've wound up in Babylon or Egypt. Your family and friends all appear to be of the mindset that it is your fault. You are where you are because of your own doing. Yet after much prayer and self-examination you know that it's not your fault. Then you are likely being tested. So what's next.

First of all be assured that God is not sleeping he is well aware of your situation and has cleared it from the very throne room of glory. He has allowed the test. You should also know that with the help of the Holy Spirit you will pass with flying colors. As Job *stated when He has tried me, I shall come forth as gold.* Not only are you going to pass the test but you'll come out glowing, shining as precious gold. The other thing to remember is not to fear, because God is your source and protection. You may be right at the gates of Hell City or as scripture says *Satan's seat.* Hang in there help is on the way. So how are you going to take your test? Are you going to moan and complain? Are you going to blame others? Are you going to become afraid? Or are you going to dig in and stand strong? Here are a few suggestions.

10

Don't worry, be happy!!!

(Philippians 4:4) Rejoice in *the* Lord always. Again I say, Rejoice!(James 1:2) My brothers, count *it* all joy when you fall into different kinds of temptations,
(John 16:33) I have spoken these things to you so that you might have peace in Me. In the world you shall have tribulation, but be of good cheer. I have overcome the world.

Remember that song a few years back that simple little song that said *don't worry be happy!!!* God's word instructs us to always rejoice, count it all joy, and to be of good cheer. Therefore in the midst of our bondage when we are being tried and tested our demeanor should be one of contentment. Not only that, we should be cheerful. I remember Bishop Rance Allen preaching a sermon some years back entitled simply "Cheer Up". It is only through God that we can reach this state in the midst of tough times. *You will keep him in perfect peace, whose mind is stayed on You; because he trusts in You. (Isaiah 26:3)* When we trust God and not our circumstances, then we are able to be cheerful while at the same time being tried and tested. Keep the promises of God along with a song in your heart. Know that your troubles are just for a period of time a season.

Be Still: (Exodus 14:13) And Moses said to the people, Do not fear. Stand still and see the salvation of Jehovah, which He will prepare for you this day. For the Egyptians whom you have seen today, you shall never see them anymore.
It may appear that you will never break out or break free. It may appear that you are closed in or bound for life. Your situation may appear hopeless. Yet there is God!!! All that you have to do is just stand still and while you are standing still you'll see the salvation of the Lord. He's going to show up and show out in a mighty way. Not only that, some of your accusers and detractors. You're not going to see them anymore. There are people that have grieved your very spirit, you will never in life see them anymore not alone

11

deal with them. That's enough to stop right now and give God some praise. God's going to take you out of Egypt and Babylon and take you to your destiny in this life.

(Joshua 10:12) Then Joshua spoke to Jehovah in the day when Jehovah delivered up the Amorites before the sons of Israel, and he said in the sight of Israel, Sun! Stand still on Gibeon! And, moon, *stand still* in the valley of Aijalon!
(Joshua 10:13) And the sun stood still, and the moon stood *still*, until the people *had* avenged themselves on their enemies. *Is* this not written in the Book of Jasher? And the sun stood *still* in the midst of the heavens, and did not hasten to go down about a whole day.
(Joshua 10:14) And there was no day like that before it or after it, that Jehovah listened to the voice of a man. For Jehovah fought for Israel.

God is going to allow you to speak some things into existence. He's going to put you in situations where people are going to have to deal with you. Things are going to happen according to your wishes because God is going to back you up. People will not be able to get around you or pass you over. It's going to be amazing how things turn out. If God can empower Joshua to where the sun and the moon stood still. Think about what he's capable of doing in your current situation. It is going to be awesome folks are going to have to deal with you on your terms. It may be banks, corporations, states, cities, whatever your situation when God shows up victory is guaranteed. In your own special way you need to give God praise for what he is about to do just for you and you alone.

(Psalms 46:10) Be still, and know that I am God! I will be praised among the nations, I will be praised in the earth. Realize that God is God over everything he is not going to let you down. He cannot or will not fail. God is going to work things out for you because he is God. Your victory will be a testament to the truth of his word and his promises. The end is already set and you win.

12

Yes we all win in the end through Jesus Christ but God also wants us to win in this life. Our detractors, our accusers, and those secretly plotting against us, they will all see the mighty hand of God bring about victory for us in this life.

What they did behind closed doors, on the internet, over cell phones Instagram and Facebook. God's going to overturn it in a manner that all will see. He's going to raise you up and put you out in front of everyone who falsely accused you. Everyone who set traps for you forcing you into bondage. Once God sets you free you are going to be free. As I shared with you earlier you won't even have to see or deal with some of those people ever again in life. They'll be watching you on CNN or Lifestyles of the Truly, wonderfully, and Marvelously Blessed (in other words you're going to be BIGG NEWS by the way I wrote this before our current president spoke how big things were going to be).

You Must Protect Your House!!!
(Ephesians 6:10) Finally, my brothers, be strong in *the* Lord and in the power of His might.
(Ephesians 6:11) Put on the whole armor of God so that you may be able to stand against the wiles of the devil.
(Ephesians 6:12) For we do not wrestle against flesh and blood, but against principalities, against powers, against the world's rulers, of the darkness of this age, against spiritual wickedness in high *places*.
(Ephesians 6:13) Therefore take to yourselves the whole armor of God, that you may be able to withstand in the evil day, and having done all, to stand.

Whenever you find yourself in trouble whether from your own doing or just the tests and trials of this life. You must learn how to take care of yourself. Satan is playing for keeps and he wants to destroy you and those that you love and care for. Just as the Under Armor commercial used to say *we must protect this house.* That is what you must do, protect your house.

Your, physical, emotional, and spiritual house all must be protected. Protecting your house will take strength and that strength comes from God in his power and might. Our strength can wilt under the constant attack of satan. However with the help of the Holy Spirit and through determination resulting from our trust in God and not our situations then we can make it. Your fight is not with people but with the satanic forces that influence them.

This is why it is so important that you are truly ready for battle and fully equipped to fight the forces of evil. You must put on the whole armor of God. This includes prayer through prayer you establish a meaningful relationship with God. Faith that is strong and unshakable showing that you are trusting in God and not your circumstances. You study God's word, not just read it; you dig deeper to uncover its truths in order that they become evident in your daily walk. You take on a Godly lifestyle where people can see that there is something different in you. One way to become stronger is to rid yourself of the constant negative memories of your past.

Once you have overcome your past mentally then you can find your path towards freedom. After you have found your way then you must help others to find their way out of bondage. Once you have found your path and help others to find theirs then you can live a life in true victory and freedom. Your freedom provides you with the ability and privilege to serve others. You find that life is meaningful and full as you find joy through impacting the lives of others. The first step is to rid yourself of the mistakes of the past

GETTING PAST YOUR PAST

Self -examination
(Psalms 139:23) Search me, O God, and know my heart; try me, and know my thoughts,
(Psalms 139:24) and see if *any* wicked way *is* in me; and lead me in the way everlasting.

(Ezra 4:15) so that search may be made in the book of the records of your fathers, and you shall find in the book of the records, and shall know that *this* city *is* a rebellious city, hurtful to kings and provinces, and that they have rebelled in it in the past, for which cause that city was destroyed.

Many of us are faced with constantly dealing with the mistakes, habits, or various problems from our past. Sometimes those that are dearest to us, help to constantly remind us of our past failures. Often they are not even aware of the added hurt and pain that it causes us to constantly be reminded of past failures or mistakes.

Each New Year we hope to make a fresh start hoping to put the past behind us only to once again be reminded of our past at some point during the year. God wants us to live in peace God wants to permanently free us from our past. However there are steps that we should take in order to prepare ourselves for the mental security and freedom that only the Holy Spirit can provide.

First we must honestly examine ourselves. Then we should seek the Holy Spirit's guidance as to what is unpleasing in the sight of God. It could be something that we have not resolved from our past. We may also have something in our lives right at this moment that the Holy Spirit needs to rid us of. Once we have allowed the Holy Spirit to rid us of whatever is hindering us and keeping us from freedom. Once we have truly repented of our past as well as current short comings, then and only then can we move forward. Notice how the psalmist David inquires of God to search his heart and mind. Then he asks for guidance in the right direction. Once God through his Holy Spirit has cleansed us then we can move on.

The next step is to examine our own personal environment. If you notice in Ezra 4:15 that the actions of the people's ancestors, brought about the destruction of the city and the prophet points this fact out to the people. God forgives sin, however he does not accept, tolerate, or understand sin. It is only because of grace that it appears that he tolerates sin. He often does not deal with us as he should. However when God has enough, he has had enough. Then we face his judgment or chastisement.

If we are honest with ourselves we can look back and see how God dealt with sin in our family tree as well as those we associate with. Sin often shortens the lives of those who continue to live a life in rebellion to God's word. Rebellion is crazy when it is against the mandates of God. Who can withstand the chastisement and wrath of God? No one can defeat God, as stated when God says that enough it really is over. The consequences for rebelling against God can prove fatal. Sin is rebelling and when we sin we rebel, thus opening ourselves up for God's wrath or correction.

Sins of the Past
((Ecclesiastes 3:16) And again I saw under the sun the place of judgment, that wickedness *was* there; and the place of righteousness, that wickedness *was* there.
(Ecclesiastes 3:17) I said in my heart, God shall judge the righteous and the wicked; for *there is* a time there for every purpose and for every work.
(Jeremiah 8:19) Behold the voice of the cry of the daughter of my people, from a far country. *Is* not Jehovah in Zion? *Is* not her King in her? Why have they provoked Me with their graven images, with foreign vanities
(Jeremiah 8:20) The harvest is past, the summer is ended, and we are not saved.
(Jeremiah 8:21) For the breaking of the daughter of my people I am broken; I am in gloom; horror has seized me.
(Jeremiah 8:22) *Is there* no balm in Gilead? Is there no physician there? Why then has the healing of the daughter of My people not come?

16

(Act 14:16) who in past generations allowed all nations to walk in their *own* ways.

(Act 14:17) And yet He did not leave Himself without witness, doing good, giving rain and fruitful season to us from heaven, filling our hearts with food and gladness.

Our scripture text found in ECCLESIASTES shows us that wickedness was amongst both those who were considered righteous as well as those that were known to be wicked. The author further states that God's judgment would come upon both. We often speak of God's mercy and grace but don't want to deal with his judgment. God chastens his children just as a good parent will discipline a wayward child. When sin has entered our personal life or the lives of those around us, then we should expect God's judgment if there is no change of heart.

In our scriptures found in the book of JEREMIAH God's people are suffering as a result of years of disobedience. Read the dos and don'ts of DEUTERONOMY 28. God's people did not take heed to them therefore the results were as God had promised. Notice the reference to the seasons passing and yet the people are still in the same predicament. The prophet longs for God to heal his people. However the consequences of sin were long term and lasted for years.

Many times we question as to why those that are truly wicked appear to be blessed and fortunate. In Acts we find that God allows his good to fall on everyone to the point that entire nations were allowed to basically live their own godless lives and still be blessed. So you may ask then why am I going through what I'm going through? One reason is because when we as Christians sin as mentioned before. God chastens or disciplines us because of our disobedience. For those who do not know God they will face an eternity of punishment for their lack of Faith in God along with their wrong doing. At some point before they leave this earth God will also deal with them. He corrects us so that we will return to him and once again follow his guidance.

When we are truly honest with ourselves we know when we are being tested and when God is chastening us. Sometimes we grow weary of both. Notice how Jeremiah longs for God's healing. The *harvest is past, the summer is ended and we are not saved* he quotes. Why not think about it; summer and fall periods where we see growth and then reap the abundance from the growth. Yet Jeremiah says that they are not saved. Yes the seasons have changed yet their season of suffering has not. What an awful place to be in all because of their sins.

Notice how he inquires as to whether or not there is a balm in Gilead, in other words is there no cure or medicine for our predicament? Even a little salve to numb the pain. Then he goes on to ask is there no physician or is there a doctor in the house? Unlike the saints of old who needed lambs and goats to sacrifice because of their sins. We have instant help ready to act once we act.

NEW LIFE THROUGH CHRIST
(Eph 2:1) And He *has made you alive*, who were once dead in trespasses and sins,
(Eph 2:2) in which you once walked according to the course of this world, according to the prince of the power of the air, the spirit that now works in the children of disobedience;
(Eph 2:3) among whom we also had our way of life in times past, in the lusts of our flesh, fulfilling the desires of the flesh and of the thoughts, and were by nature the children of wrath, even as others.
(Eph 2:4) But God, who is rich in mercy, for His great love *with* which He loved us
(Son 2:11) For lo, the winter is past, the rain is over; it goes to itself.
(Son 2:12) the flowers appear on the earth; the time of singing has come, and the voice of the turtle-dove is heard in our land;

Because of the perfection of Calvary all we have to do is repent. For the unsaved all you have to do is accept the perfect gift of salvation along with repentance. Allow Jesus to become Lord of your life. For the backsliding Christian, just give up and give in. God wants full control of your life not partial control, he wants to drive. Not just sometime but all of the time. Notice our scripture God has made us alive through the perfect work of Calvary. We are to become dead to our old sins of the past. Every sinful thought or habit that came to us naturally has to go. Satan sets the agenda for this world in our scripture he is referred to as the prince of the power of the air. When we think of air it is not a visible substance. It does not provide us with anything tangible to hold on to yet we feel its affects. The same with sin we can't see sin visibly however we feel, also experience the affects and results of sin.

Calvary delivered us from sin, Jesus came to die for us in order that sin would no longer have rule and reign over us. We are no longer to participate in what the world looks upon as normal. We become abnormal to the world's way of thinking. Sin is no longer a natural part of our lives. We have a new agenda one that is opposite to that we once had. Look at our scripture in our fleshly desires of the past we were referred to as children of wrath. In other words our daily sinful lives brought God to anger.

He was very displeased with us to the point that we drew his wrath. Now because of Christ we are on his good side. Look at our scriptures from the Song of Solomon. The winter is gone spring has sprung flowers are blooming birds are singing even the voice of the turtle-dove is heard throughout the land. In others words Christ has taken away the pain of our past and given us a song to sing.

(2Pe 1:4) through which He has given to us exceedingly great and precious promises, so that by these you might be partakers of *the* divine nature, having escaped the corruption *that is* in *the* world through lust.
(2Pe 1:5) But also in this very thing, bringing in all diligence, filling out your faith with virtue, and with virtue, knowledge;

19

(2Pe 1:6) and *with* knowledge self-control, and *with* self-control, patience, and *with* patience, godliness,
(2Pe 1:7) and *with* godliness, brotherly kindness, and *with* brotherly kindness, love.
(2Pe 1:8) For if these things are in you and abound, they make *you to be* neither idle nor unfruitful in the knowledge of our Lord Jesus Christ.
2Pe 1:9) For *he* in whom these things are not present is blind and cannot see afar off and has forgotten that he was purged from his sins in the past.
(2Pe 1:10) Therefore, brothers, rather be diligent to make your calling and election sure, for *if you* do these things, you shall never fall.

Once we allow the Holy Spirit full control of our lives we take on a divine nature. As the scripture tells us we escape the corruption that is in the world through lust. There should be a noticeable difference in how we speak, talk, and act. We must be honest with ourselves, what attributes have we taken on. Does our daily life reflect that we now walk in faith, with virtue, knowledge, self-control, patience, godliness, brotherly kindness, and love? Which of these attributes are we lacking?   It is important that we examine ourselves and allow the Holy Spirit to cleanse and purge us so that these are part of our new make-up as a person.

The scripture tells us that when they are not part of our make-up then we are blind spiritually and have forgotten that we have been purged of our past sins. Sometimes when we deal with others we forget our past short comings. Instead of being understanding and loving we are judgmental totally forgetting our own past short comings. We forget that it was because of God's grace and mercy that we survived long enough for the Holy Spirit to set us free. The scripture also assures us that when we are diligent in allowing the Holy Spirit to be in control, to the point that these attributes manifest themselves in our lives. We are assured that we will never fall.

LIVING THE NEW LIFE

(Heb 12:1) Therefore since we also are surrounded with so great a cloud of witnesses, let us lay aside every weight and the sin which so easily besets *us*, and let us run with patience the race that is set before us,

(Phi 3:13) My brothers, I do not count myself to have taken possession, but one *thing I do*, forgetting the things behind and reaching forward to the things before,

(Phi 3:14) I press toward the mark for the prize of the high calling of God in Christ Jesus.

(Phi 3:15) Let us therefore, as many as *are* perfect, be of this mind. And if in anything you are otherwise minded, God shall reveal even this to you.

(Phi 3:16) Yet, as to what we have already attained, let us walk in the same rule, let us mind the same thing.

(Phi 3:17) Brothers, be imitators together of me, and mark those who walk this way, for you have us *for* a pattern.

(Phi 3:18) (For many are walking, of whom I have told you often and now tell you even weeping, *as* the enemies of the cross of Christ;

(Phi 3:19) whose end *is* destruction, whose god *is their* belly, and *whose* glory *is* in their shame, *those* who mind earthly things.)

(Phi 3:20) For our citizenship is in Heaven, from which also we are looking for the Savior, *the* Lord Jesus Christ,

As we learn to live the life of a true follower of Christ one who is guided by the Holy Spirit. We must make sure that we do not revisit the sinful ways of our past. Our sinful lifestyle has to be permanently laid to rest. Should we falter or fall we must allow the Holy Spirit to pick us back up and continue to move forward. We should look at those who portray the attributes stated earlier and pattern ourselves accordingly. If it is evident that God is in their lives then these are the type of people that we want to be around.

However if they do not exemplify Christ in their daily walk then they are actually enemies of the cross as scripture duly notes. There are some really bad people out there and even amongst those who consider themselves Christians. When they do not exemplify Christ in their daily walk then we should be wary of them.

FRUITS OF THE SPIRIT

(Gal 5:22) But the fruit of the Spirit is: love, joy, peace, long-suffering, kindness, goodness, faith,

(Gal 5:23) meekness, self-control; against such things there is no law.

(Gal 5:24) But those belonging to Christ have crucified the flesh with *its* passions and lusts.

(Gal 5:25) If we live in *the* Spirit, let us also walk in *the* Spirit.

(Gal 5:26) Let us not become glory-seeking, provoking one another, envying one another.

(Eph 5:6) Let no man deceive you with vain words, for because of these things the wrath of God comes upon the children of disobedience.

(Eph 5:7) Therefore do not be partakers with them.

(Eph 5:8) For you were once darkness, but now *you are* light in *the* Lord; walk as children of light

(Eph 5:9) For the fruit of the Spirit *is* in all goodness and righteousness and truth.

(Eph 5:10) proving what is acceptable to the Lord.

(Eph 5:11) And have no fellowship with the unfruitful works of darkness, but rather reprove *them.*

(Eph 5:12) For it is a shame even to speak of those things which are done by them in secret.

(Eph 5:13) But all things that are reproved are made manifest by the light, for whatever makes manifest *is* light.

It is very popular these days to talk about the Holy Spirit being in someone as evidenced by them speaking in tongues. Yet we often forget to mentions those attributes and characteristics of those full of the Holy Spirit. When the Holy Spirit is in control of our lives the evidence should also be found in our daily lives.

Paul in Galatians 5 along with Ephesians 5 mentions the same attributes and characteristics as Peter does. This is not by mistake, once God through his Holy Spirit is in control of our lives people should see a change. If there is no visible change reflecting what has happened on the inside. Then either we are not truly converted or we have not surrendered control to the Holy Spirit.

Not only should there be a visible change in our lives but we should also no longer desire the sinful environment of our past. The best way to get past our past is by not visiting the sinful places of our past. Sometimes that involves distancing ourselves from family and friends. Not that we are any better but because we have been delivered and set free of sin's hold on our lives.

We must even stay away from church folk who appear to have hidden agendas or do not reflect in their daily lives that the Holy Spirit is in control. It also should be noted that we should allow people to grow in Christ. They will not change overnight. However if they are supposed to be Christians and show no sign of change or become stagnant in their walk then we should limit our interaction with them. For those however, who are strong in their faith and their walk they have a responsibility to help those that are weak in their faith.

Summing things up the way to get past your past is to allow the Holy Spirit full control and reign over your life. This is something that will only happen through request. God through the Holy Spirit will not force his will on you. It is up to you through prayer and the study of God's word, that you invite and allow the Holy Spirit to take control.

The Path to Personal Freedom:

(Proverbs 16:25) There is a way that seems right to a man, but the end of it is the ways of death.

(Psalms 27:11) Teach me Your way, O Jehovah, and lead me in a plain path, because of my enemies.

(Psalms 119:105) NUN: Your Word is a lamp to my feet, and a light to my path.

Spiritual: There first thing we must do as we journey through life is to realize which direction to go. If we look at life as a journey that takes us along various paths then we want to always be sure that we take the right one. As far as the path to personal freedom it starts once you honestly examine your personal situation and yourself. Once you have dealt with the past and other things that have you bound or are hindering your progress then you are on your way. The true path to freedom may not be as clear as one might think.

In our first scripture found in Proverbs we find someone who honestly feels that they are on the right path only to be headed towards death. Just turn on the television these days and you'll find programming that for all intents and purposes appears to be good but will lead you down the path to death. For example the very popular sitcom the *Golden Girls. H*ere we have a group of single middle aged to senior citizen ladies. They are very loving and caring women with what on first glance appears to be good morals and values. Yet on closer examination they are far from it when we apply biblical standards. This statement will shock some but in fact they are all whores. Why? Because all of them in one episode or another engaged in sex outside of the sanctity of marriage even the oldest one.

They practiced a lifestyle of sexual immorality. Sex is reserved and even commanded for those that are married no matter what the age. To live a lifestyle that incorporates sex outside of marriage is one that is sinful. It is one thing to make a mistake and fail morally as we all do because we are still tempted and subject to the failures of the flesh. However if you are daily living a lifestyle contrary to the word then you are on the wrong

24

path and headed for death (an early one due to sin). So you think that the *Golden Girls* were cute and sassy for their ages. The statistics are staggering when it comes to HIV positive women over age 50. This age group saw a 107% increase since 1991 (http://aids.about.com/cs/aidsfactsheets/a/olderhiv.htm). We won't just pick on the *Golden Girls, Sex in the City, Will & Grace, the L-word, Desperate House Wives* all of these programs foster a lifestyle that can literally send you to an early exit from this life. So Hollywood is not where one should look when searching for their path to personal freedom. (Please note I first wrote this book around 2006 things have gotten a whole lot worst) In my opinion I believe often times movies tell stories however TV shows or series and now even the internet. I believe they often foster the promotion of a hidden agenda. This is done to inforce society to accept a certain type of lifestyle, political agenda etc.

Teach me Your way, O Jehovah, and lead me in a plain path, because of my enemies. The psalmist David has it right we are to seek the guidance of the Holy Spirit if we are to take the proper pathway towards freedom. *Your Word is a lamp to my feet, and a light to my path.* Here again the psalmist has it right God's Holy word the Bible will shine its light into our spirit showing us the right path to take.

The Practical: *(Leviticus 11:2) Speak to the sons of Israel, saying, These are the animals which you shall eat among all the animals that are in the earth.* For years it has been said that the do's and don'ts of this chapter were not applicable for us today. The reason being that after Peter's vision where he was instructed to rise and eat what up until that time had been food forbidden by law, his vision was a license for us to literally pig out. Experts and nutritionist who have studied the Bible have found that many of the foods that were forbidden in the Old Testament. Should be forbidden in our daily diets not because of the Mosaic laws but because they actually are not good for human consumption.

True personal freedom incorporates sound decision making in every aspect of our lives. We should also be health conscious as well as spiritually aware on a daily basis. God is a healer and worker of miracles even now. It is crazy to ask God to heal you of cancer then go out and buy a carton of cigarettes. Especially when the doctor tells you that you're cancer free. I remember my dad (even though he was blessed with longevity) after recovering from a stroke he was cooking a sausage patty the size of a whopper in a skillet full of grease.

Today our air quality is poor, our food is unnatural, and we consume too much of everything that is bad for us. We must become better stewards of our bodies as far as what we eat and how we take care of it. Exercise should be part of our daily routine along the path towards freedom take out the time daily to take a walk literally. You may not be able to afford to work out in the latest gym or fitness center. Walking and pushups are free.

Financially it just makes good sense to plan ahead. Sometimes you are better off either not having something or waiting until you can purchase it in cash. Planning ahead and establishing a rainy day fund for emergencies just makes good sense. If you are able to work then you are able to save. One of the worst forms of bondage is that of financial bondage. The Lord's Prayer instructs of to forgive our debts as we forgive our debtors. Somehow we forget this section in today's society and usury something the Bible instructs us not to give our money to is common place.

You find it in credit cards 22% interest rates when you read the fine print. Those pay day cash advance places, buy here pay here car loans. You might be better off saving your money and paying cash for a car. Ride a bike and use public transportation until you can afford to pay cash. Home ownership without burdening yourself with too much debt when it comes to buying one can be very rewarding. There is a sense of accomplishment and liberty when your house is your home and you own it.

Once you have gotten it together and are on the right track then you have an obligation to help others. So often it has been said by some that they got theirs on their own so others must do the same. However you never really do it on your own it is through God's grace and mercy that you make it to personal freedom. If Christ had not chosen to lay down his life for us where would we be? Selfishness is not a characteristic of a Christian. When following the example of the savior we realize that our needs come last when we have the opportunity to help others. So once you break free and are successfully on the path of personal freedom then it is your moral obligation to help others.

Showing others the path to freedom:

(1Peter 5:10) But the God of all grace, He calling us to His eternal glory by Christ Jesus, after you have suffered a little, He will perfect, confirm, strengthen, and establish you.
(Luke 22:32) But I have prayed for you, that your faith fail not. And when you are converted, strengthen your brothers.
(Leviticus 25:35) And if your brother has become poor, and his hand has failed with you, then you shall help him; yes, even if he is a stranger or a tenant, so that he may live with you.
(Deu 22:4) You shall not see your brother's ass or his ox fall down by the way, and hide yourself from them. You shall surely help him to lift it up again.
(Ecc 4:9) Two are better than one; because they have a good reward for their labor.
(Ecc 4:10) For if they fall, the one will lift up his fellow; but woe to him who is alone when he falls, for he does not have another to help him.

In the word God promises to *perfect, confirm, strengthen, and establish* us. So by faith through grace we are going to get there. Once we are there once we have been set free then we are to in turn show others the path to freedom which starts at Calvary. When we point people to Jesus we point them to the path of freedom.

Helping others starts right at home. As parents we are responsible for helping our children, spiritually, emotionally, and physically. Often times when there is something lacking in your life it will continue on to your children. However you have the opportunity to stop certain things from passing from one generation to another.

If your parents had a drinking problem then maybe you should stay totally away from alcohol. If you were a product of abuse or divorce then you should pray that much harder for your marriage and go the extra mile. If you grew up with nothing, yet have a little more than your parents did then you should do everything in your power to make sure that your children have more then you. In every aspect of life do all that you can to make sure that your

children have more than you do. If you don't break the chains help
them to break them.
*(Proverbs 13:22) A good man leaves an inheritance to his sons'
sons, and the wealth of the sinner is laid up for the just.* Don't
stop at just helping yours, God wants you to help others outside of
your immediate family.

We are also to help others tangibly when there is a need and we
can provide that need it is our moral responsibility to do so. How
often do we as Christians try to avoid the knowledge of our fellow
brothers and sisters needs? If we see someone we know literally
stranded do we go and help them or do we go another way so that
we can do whatever was on our agenda at the time? Scripture tells
us that we should stop and help. Even on Sundays when we see
someone in need we should stop and help even if that means being
late or missing service all together. Even if you are the pastor or
musician maybe this Sunday God wants you to stop and minister to
that person in need that's why we have cell phones today.

 Make the call and call for help, then go on to service.
Another point is that we can't and shouldn't always do things by
ourselves. There was a reason that Jesus sent out the disciples in
couples. We need each other for help, companionship as well as
the need for advice. Whenever you can get good help you should
take advantage of it. Even when you are mentoring or helping to
show someone the way out, involve others who are knowledgeable
or who may have traveled the same path but are now free. Don't
let your personal pride prevent you from helping someone gain
their freedom call up the reserves.

Dealing with the devil:
*(Luke 8:29) (For He had commanded the unclean spirit to come
out of the man. For oftentimes it had seized him. And he had been
kept bound in chains and in fetters, and he broke the bands and
was driven into the deserted places by the demons.)*
There are cases when a person is bound literally due to demonic
possession or influence. It is not fashionable these days to admit
that satan is real even in some churches. Boy does satan like that.

It makes his job so much easier. I truly believe that there are individuals who are being held back even bound due to demonic influence or possession. It may be from demons that have been around their family for centuries in the form of what is commonly called generational curses.

There are some in the body of Christ who do not believe in generational curses. For those of you who feel this way consider this. Demons don't die or retire they have been around for centuries. *(Acts 13:10) and said, O son of the Devil, full of all deceit and all craftiness, enemy of all righteousness, will you not stop perverting the right ways of the Lord?* Satan deceives those who don't believe that he can affect generations one after the other. This scripture shows us that he is crafty so in other words he's not stupid. The people in this scripture were acting under the influence of satan. As stated demons don't die or retire and they aren't dumb.

Therefore if they were successful with your ancestors leading them into a sinful lifestyle or binding them. Then why would they stop trying because you come along. If it worked on Grand Daddy it may work on you. Satan and his buddies must be cast out in the name of Jesus they won't come out on their own. There is nothing nice about satan. He has no problem touching babies not alone adults. He'll touch a newborn and won't have any regrets or remorse.

Some might ask why, would God allow such a thing to happen. Well it is not God's desire or fault, nor is he powerless. Satan gets his power from us going back to Adam and Eve. It may be something as simple as a small lie (by the way there is no such thing a lie is a lie) that provides satan with the opportunity to raise havoc.

Whenever we are helping others we need to consult the Holy Spirit that it might reveal to us what is going on. Sometimes the bondage is demonic possession or influence and satan must be cast out of

the person or situation before freedom and restoration can take place. If demonic possession or influence is the case then you need to be real with yourself. Are you fortified and spiritually strong enough to deal with demons because they don't play? *(Acts 19:13) And certain from the strolling Jews, exorcists, undertook to name the name of the Lord Jesus over those having evil spirits, saying, We adjure you by Jesus whom Paul preaches. (Acts 19:14) And there were seven sons of Sceva, a Jewish chief priest, who did so.*
(Acts 19:15) But answering the evil spirit said, Jesus I know, and I comprehend Paul, but who are you?
(Act 19:16) And the man in whom the evil spirit resided leaped on them, and overcoming them he was strong against them, so that they fled out of the house naked and wounded.
Need I say more? Satan is nobody to play with he is jealous of all mankind because we have one thing that he'll never have and that is salvation through Jesus Christ. Don't try to cast out demons in anybody unless you are fortified spiritually and have the anointing of God's Holy Spirit and it is evident in your daily walk. Satan will tear you up and the demon that you are trying to cast out of someone else may attack you.

We have power to cast out demons in the name of Jesus. If you are weak in your faith or walk you need to call for help from other saints, those who are not only talking the talk but walking the walk. When the fruits of the Holy Spirit are manifested in a person's life those are the type of people you want praying for those under demonic influence or possession.

When the Binds are too tight!!!

(Matthew 19:6) Therefore they are no longer two, but one flesh.
Therefore what God has joined together, let not man separate.
(Mark 10:8) And the two of them shall be one flesh. So then they
are no longer two, but one flesh.

I was just about to finish this book and it was impressed upon me
to address another form of bondage. A form that is sadly found in
the institution of marriage. Husbands and wives are to become as
one according to scripture. Their marriage covenant is so strong
that they cease to be two individuals, instead they merge into one.
Sadly however in some marriages this is not the case. Instead of a
new person evolving out of the marriage union we see a form of
bondage. This bondage can come early in a marriage or even after
10, 20, or 30 years. What should be a harmonious and perfect
union is instead a stifling and binding arrangement. One that lacks
freedom.

One of the most common things being said these days when it
comes to divorce is that God wants us happy. So when couples are
no longer happy then divorce is acceptable because God wants us
happy. What God wants is OBEDIENCE. One of the main
reasons that marriages don't make it, even amongst Christian
couples is because of disobedience. The husband, the wife, or both
refuse to obey God's mandates for the marriage union. Herein lies
the root problem in many cases. Disobedience is sin and sin
breeds more sin. The key to a successful marriage is to obey
God's word.

(Eph 5:28) So men ought to love their wives as their own bodies.
He who loves his wife loves himself
(Eph 5:29) For no man ever yet hated his own flesh, but
nourishes and cherishes it, even as the Lord loves the church.

Let us start with the men first since God created us first and then
women came out of us. The scripture says that men ought to love
their wives as their own bodies. You can ask a lot of men whether
they love their wives in this manner and they would respond in the

affirmative, lying all the time. In fact what they love is the convenience of having a wife. Someone to dump on and vent on. Someone to make public appearances with and help them keep up their image. In some cases their wife is not a true part of their own personal essence. She is not really physically and spiritually their missing link. The two of them are not truly one as scripture says they should be, sadly to say she may be merely an object or sperm deposit. Just as you deposit money into a checking account so that you can spend it. Unlike a saving account or stocks that you invest in, looking forward to a return because you have made a wise and sound investment. They only put in so that they can turn around and take out.

The scripture instructs men to cherish and to nourish their wives. Men should remember that wives are like precious stones or metals that are beyond price or value. She is more valuable than anything in this life because things can be replaced she can't. Yes you can find another woman or another wife but they aren't her especially when she's God sent. *(Proverbs 31:10) Who can find a woman of virtue? For her value is far above rubies.*
(Pro 31:11) The heart of her husband trusts safely in her, so that he shall have no need of plunder.
(Pro 31:12) She will do him good and not evil all the days of her life.
How often do we find a good Godly woman married to a true character? All she wants is to please him and be a good wife and mother. Yet she is the last thing on his mind. Scripture instructs husbands to love their wives and treat them as they would treat themselves. However they may show more attention and affection to their cars or their dog or their buddies. If you are a man reading this and this fits you then God through the Holy Spirit wants to deliver you and help you become the man that he created you to be. He wants to free you from the chains that you have chosen.

(1Co 7:2) But, because of the fornications, let each have his own wife, and let each have her own husband.
(1Co 7:3) Let the husband give to the wife proper kindness, and likewise the wife also to the husband.

(1Co 7:4) The wife does not have authority over her own body, but the husband. And likewise also the husband does not have authority over his own body, but the wife.
(1Co 7:5) Do not deprive one another, unless it is with consent for a time, so that you may give yourselves to fasting and prayer. And *come together again so that Satan does not tempt you for your incontinence.*

These verses hit home today just as they did when the apostle Paul wrote them centuries ago. As stated sex is for those that are married that being a man and a woman. There is no other situation according to scripture that it is allowable in. Yet sadly in today's society sex is taking place everywhere else except the marriage bed. It is safe to say that one reason for the high divorce rate is because some married couples aren't satisfied with each other in the bedroom. This is because satan has taken control of the marriage bed. Couples are listening to Hollywood and letting the world dictate what constitutes a satisfying sex life. Let's kill that lie right now.

First of all God created sex, not satan. Just as everything else that God created sex was and is good in the confines of marriage. When people are misled into believing that sexual experiences outside of marriage are more fulfilling then those in marriage. They are being deceived big time. There is no way that a sinful experience can be more fulfilling then one that is sanctioned and ordained by God. The person believing that sinful sex is more pleasurable then that ordained by God is still being influenced by satan. They have unresolved sin in their lives and have not truly repented of past sexual sin.

Your husband or your wife can be more satisfying and provide you intimacy and pleasures beyond your wildest dreams or imagination. The reason that you have not experienced it is simple. It is YOU!!!
YOU!!! are the problem your husband or your wife doesn't need any books or he or she doesn't need to change this or that about themselves. YOU!!! however need JESUS. It amazes me how

people can have a great husband or wife who loves them and accepts them even with all of their issues and short comings.

Yet the person who is being accepted by their husband or wife, they feel that they should have someone more appealing or satisfying. How crazy is that? I see it all the time, the person with most of the issues in a marriage they talk a good game. They will be the first to say you know it's not about me but in reality it is. If this is you then you should feel blessed that you have a husband or wife someone that will put up with and take your mess. In actuality you don't deserve him or her and maybe for them the grass maybe greener on the other side. Because you have serious problems. Then there is the blame game. It is crazy how one spouse can have affairs and just do the other any kind of way and once they are found out beg and plead for forgiveness, wanting to keep the marriage together. Then the other spouse may have a lapse of judgment one time and the one who had numerous affairs becomes so hurt and wants a divorce. Jesus addressed this while not in the context of marriage, but when it comes to judging others period.

(Mat 7:3) And why do you look on the splinter that is in your brother's eye, but do not consider the beam that is in your own eye?
(Mat 7:4) Or how will you say to your brother, Let me pull the splinter out of your eye; and, behold, a beam is in your own eye?
(Mat 7:5) Hypocrite! First cast the beam out of your own eye, and then you shall see clearly to cast the splinter out of your brother's eye.
If more husbands and wives would read this scripture before they start playing the blame game there would be fewer arguments as well as divorces.

(Mal 2:13) And this is a second thing you have done, covering the altar of Jehovah with tears, weeping, and groaning, yet not facing toward the food offering, and taking it with delight from your hand.
(Mal 2:14) Yet you say. Why? Because Jehovah has been witness between you and the wife of your youth, against whom

you have dealt treacherously; yet she is your companion and your covenant wife.
(Mal 2:16) "I hate divorce," says the LORD God of Israel. "I hate it when one of you does such a cruel thing to his wife. Make sure that you do not break your promise to be faithful to your wife."
How sad it is when one spouse or the other wants to call it quits after 20 or 30 years of marriage not because of infidelity but because they just no longer want to be married as is common these days. Women are becoming just as guilty of this just as much as men these days.

Most marriages could stand the test of time if both parties were obedient to God first as stated earlier. Also if both parties are realistic, marriage is two imperfect people coming together to form a perfect union with the help of the Holy Spirit. However Hollywood and society sets unrealistic examples for marriage. Marriage like many other things in life is a growth process where two people navigate through life as one. In many cases the spouse looking for something better won't find it because in reality they are the problem. Moving on to someone else doesn't work because they didn't deal with their issues. While the other spouse who didn't want the divorce is free to move on the one who wanted it is still bound. God really hates divorce and wants couples to seek him and allow the Holy Spirit to fix their marriages. Yet in today's society we must be realistic in some cases divorce is the best option. Marriages where there is physical abuse are one example and where there is infidelity is another. Usually where there is one there is also the other and God does allow for divorce when there is infidelity in the marriage. In both cases the victim could wind up dead.

(Gen 3:6) The woman saw how beautiful the tree was and how good its fruit would be to eat, and she thought how wonderful it would be to become wise. So she took some of the fruit and ate it. Then she gave some to her husband, and he also ate it.

This is how things got messed up in the first place due to a woman looking with the wrong set of eyes. When satan got Eve's attention and she looked at the fruit he was in, and sin then entered paradise.

The look caused Eve to sin. Today more women than ever are being unfaithful and that is because satan is using men to get their attention and to look with the wrong set of eyes. The natural eye is subject to the flesh while if we look at things through the eyes of the Holy Spirit then we can see the truth.

At times married women feel that their husbands don't give them enough time or attention. So when another man or in today's society another woman comes along and shows them some attention. They fall victim to satan once again, just as Eve did. When your husband doesn't give you the proper attention or spend quality time with you then pray that much harder for him. Then you must put on the whole armor of God because satan and his demons smell blood. They can sense an opportunity to take you down. I often tell people that you don't have to be alone with anyone in a place where the opportunity to commit adultery could occur. God always provides a means of escape when we fall into sexual sin it is our choice.

(Hebrews 13:4) Marriage is honorable in all, and the bed undefiled, but fornicators and adulterers God will judge.
Bringing this section to a close God wants married couples to be happy and truly enjoy each other. However society today paints a picture that marriage and monogamy are boring even outdated. Yet scripture tells us that God is going to judge the fornicators and adulterers. At the same time he provides the married couple with freedom in the bedroom. How novel that married couples can enjoy each other and not feel guilty.

Earlier I shared scripture where both husband and wife were made aware of the fact that once married the husband's body belongs to the wife and the wife's body belongs to the husband. Therefore neither party has the right to share their body with someone other than their spouse. So your lover in fact is a thief they are enjoying something that does not belong to them and you are giving them

37

something that you don't have the right to give. Along that line of thinking then couples should realize that they must make time to accommodate each other's physical as well as emotional needs.

Many times the one spouse who is not in the mood feels that the one who's in the mood is being selfish. Where in many cases both are being selfish at the same time, once again I believe that society and Hollywood have given us the wrong concept of sex. Married couples should have sex as often as possible for several reasons and earlier scripture encourages this. Married couples should take a fresh look and approach to sex when there is a problem in this area.

One thing both parties should do and I touched on this earlier. If there had been prior sexual experiences before marriage or adultery in the marriage there must be true repentance. Repentance frees you of the sexual bondage that prevents you from really enjoying and appreciating your spouse for who they are. When you compare your spouse to prior immoral sexual experiences then you have not truly repented and are yet bound. You cannot truly enjoy or appreciate your spouse until you have asked God to cleanse and purge you of your past sexual sins and desires. When you can look on your past sexual sins with disgust, hating the fact that they ever happened then you have reached a point of freedom. Once this happens then you can experience the joys of your spouse in ways that you never imagined.

There are three areas that I want to focus on when it comes to the marriage bedroom. First of all sex is for reproduction as commanded by God in Genesis the second chapter and again in the ninth chapter man is told to be fruitful and multiply. Second when we consider that man and woman no longer are two but one flesh. Then we realize that the coming together is more than reproduction and sexual fulfillment. In the scriptures quoted earlier Paul instructs husbands and wives *(1Co 7:5) Do not deprive one another, unless it is with consent for a time, so that you may give yourselves to fasting and prayer. And come together again so that Satan does not tempt you for your incontinence.*

If a husband and wife refrain from sex in order to focus on fasting and prayer then when they come together again something more than the physical has to take place. This is a concept that I call sexual communion. The word communion means- *the act or an instance of sharing, as of thoughts or feelings or spiritual fellowship.* It is taken from the Latin word *commun-i-o* which means mutual participation. I could stop right there you see mutually both husband and wife decide to devote time to fasting and prayer and then mutually *come together again.* This has to be an awesome experience because the sex act now takes on a more spiritual aspect.

This is why Paul encourages them to come together again so that Satan does not tempt you for your incontinence. Satan hates a couple like this because they are a threat to him. This type of couple has Christ right in the center of their marriage. They can do awesome work for the Lord because they truly are one in the spirit and the flesh. This type of couple can experience things sexually that others can only dream of, which brings us to our final point.

Finally we have sex between husband and wife for the sheer and mutual enjoyment of each other. Just as in the concept of sexual communion the sex act is one of mutual agreement and enjoyment. Both husband and wife are enjoying and pleasing each other. Depending on what stage their marriage is in couples should schedule time to experience each category that we've described. There are times when couples say that the passion or spark is gone from their sex life. My response is that passion and sparks are temporary.

You can experience both to a degree in an ungodly relationship. What you want is a fire, constant warmth; your sex life should be as natural as breathing. However correct breathing as most vocal coaches will tell you takes proper technique, practice, and work. The same can be said for the married couple's sex life. God in his

Holy word has given you freedom in your bedroom it is up to you as a couple to exercise that freedom.

Note: I first published this book in 2006 since that time I've written another book devoted entirely to marriage entitled *How Two Become One.* **The more I study scripture the more I realize that God really does hate divorce under any circumstances. Yet I saw a recent poll where atheists had a better record than Christians when it came to marriage and divorce. It is ever so important that Christians exercise both Prayer and Patience when it comes to marriage. As my dad often said you can wait until you are 61 to get married and if you marry the wrong person you've married a day too soon. God intended for marriage to be life long and that death be the only thing that brought about permanent separation of husband and wife.**

At the same I do not believe that God wants someone to stay in a marriage that is abusive. Nor do I believe he wants someone to stay in a marriage where there is constant infidelity. All that being said much, much prayer should be made before and constantly throughout marriage. Intense prayer should be made before you file for divorce.

Finally and we're done on the topic of marriage. I believe that scripture clearly defines marriage as being that of a woman and a man. God willing in another offering we'll go much deeper on the topic of sexuality as well as same sex marriage. If you are reading this book or eBook and would like for me to go deeper email me minister8mike@yahoo.com **I'll be glad to respond.**

Freedom to serve:

(*Romans 7:6*) But now we having been set free from the Law, having died *to that* in which we were held, so that we serve in newness of spirit and not *in* oldness of the letter.
Because of the perfect work of Calvary we are no longer bound to our past sins or mistakes. God has forgiven us and cast our sins into the sea of forgetfulness never to be brought up again. Our old sinful nature is gone and we now can freely serve God in a new spirit. With joy, peace, and contentment, yes we may fall or back track sometime. Yet the Holy Spirit is right there to restore us once we repent. We now find joy in serving God by serving each other.

We no longer have a selfish attitude or a mean disposition because the Holy Spirit has set us free. Over time as we walk daily with God the past will become a faint memory and true healing will take the place of hurt. You will be confident in all that you say and do because of your strong relationship with God. God wants us to enjoy life and the company of each other. Bondage is a result of sin and satan.

God through the completed work of Calvary has given us all that we need to be free in this life. Freedom is a choice Jesus Christ paid the price for our freedom. All we have to do is maintain a constant relationship with him and be a good student of his word. In doing so we can stand the tests of this life and experience a life of freedom through Jesus Christ. At the same time we can and are obligated to help others experience that same freedom.

Choose Life

(Deuteronomy 30:19) I call Heaven and earth to record today against you. I have set before you life and death, blessing and cursing. Therefore, choose life, so that both you and your seed may live,

(Deuteronomy 30:20) so that you may love Jehovah your God, and that you may obey His voice, and that you may cling to Him. For He is your life and the length of your days, so that you may dwell in the land which Jehovah swore to your fathers, to Abraham, to Isaac, and to Jacob, to give it to them.

As we come to a close of this literary offering before we end, we'd like to offer you a choice. You can choose to continue on your current path one that may be headed towards an early death. Or you can choose the path to freedom and life. In our scripture text we find that after God had given Moses the Do's and Don'ts of the 28 chapter the mosaic covenant is established in the next chapter. In the 30ᵗʰ chapter where our text is found. God now gives the children of Israel the ability to choose either life or death. That choice is still being offered today and you have the same opportunity to make that choice. There are several areas in which you can decide whether you want life or death.

Practical: As we stated earlier there are practical common sense things that you can do in order to choose life. Habits such as smoking literally deprive you of life. Smoking affects the lungs which are the airways to life. As you clog them up you stifle your own life literally. Yes you are still alive but your quality of life would improve so much if you'd stop smoking. Just simple walking everyday would also improve your health, one of the best things that you could do for your body is to take a walk. Your diet is so important to your quality of life and its longevity. You literally are what you eat. In the area of your finances making sound financial decisions will help eliminate a degree of stress in your life. A stress free life contributes to a better quality of life. Education is another choice that can improve your quality of life, learning should be lifelong and knowledge is power. I finally got my BA past age forty and found that learning at this age was very rewarding. Since then I've done everything except my thesis, working towards a MLS and also have taken seminary courses. Learning for me at this point in my life has proved to be not only rewarding but stimulating, adding quality to my life.

Emotional: Emotional stability is another positive attribute that ads quality to life as well as longevity. Nothing is better than having a sound mind and good positive relationships. We spent a lot of time dealing with marriages that have become stifling and binding instead of a maturation of two becoming one. Infidelity snatches the life out of not only the marriage but also those individuals that are affected directly or indirectly as a result of the infidelity. The sex act is a life giving act both physically and spiritually. Hollywood and society teaches that people should practice safe sex. There is no such thing as safe sex except in the confines of marriage.

Males are depositors when man and woman come together sexually. The man makes a deposit, physically, emotionally, and spiritually. He either deposits life or death in all three areas. It is possible to deposit life physically resulting in a child, yet deposit death in the other two areas. Even in marriage the man can deposit life literally and death emotionally and spiritually. That is why couples need to spend time in prayer for their marriage union along with quality time with each other. Just as the president annually makes his state of the union address. Couples need to come together and honestly report to each other the state of their union. Not playing the blame game but coming together in love in order that they might improve and strengthen their union.

Women are receptors in the sex act they literally receive what their male partner who should also be their husband puts out. They literally receive life from him every time they come together sexually. That life once conception has taken place literally breeds another life. Here in is where the myth of safe sex comes to play. When a couple come together outside of the marriage union practicing what they call safe sex then what is actually going on.

The man is not depositing any form of life into the woman only death. The woman receives no life physically, emotionally, or spiritually only death. The man is actually refusing to help you live instead he is snatching life from you.

Women are nurturers of life whether child bearing or not. Whatever the man deposits they nurture or grow. From that nurturing and growing new life is produced. When you have sexually relationships outside of marriage. Both parties become malnourished. Something is lacking and missing. That being total commitment. The man needs that nourishment that only marriage can bring. Without it he is like a vagabond wandering from one malnourished relationship after another. Neither party is whole or complete and neither one has chosen life. The oneness can only come through marriage. Marriages that are Christ centered breed life.
Ungodly relationships in any form are not life giving but life draining. They do not breed life they snatch it away.
(Amos 3:3) Can two walk together unless they are agreed?
My dad always said that his dad would say that you can't say good God and good devil. In our friendships and relationships we can't walk hand and hand in fellowship with those that are ungodly. While God will always put us in situations where we will come across those that are unsaved.

However there should be a degree of distance and a difference between us and them. Our goal should be to live a lifestyle that draws them to our Godly way of life and not theirs. We should always be cordial, kind, helpful, friendly, and accessible. We should not be hanging out together in places that as Christians we should not frequent. As Christians there are some places that we just should not go.

When we get too close to those who are ungodly or unsaved then it appears that we are in agreement with their lifestyle. At the same time we should not be so stand offish that we are of no use to them. Ask the Holy Spirit how to help and deal with them. Let God through the Holy Spirit guide you as to what is appropriate. You should also seek wise Godly counsel as to how to maintain an appropriate relationship.

Spiritually: *(Proverbs 3:6) In all your ways acknowledge Him, and He shall direct your paths.* It is just that simple invite God into your decision making process. God wants you to live and have a great quality of life. He wants you to enjoy life as well as living this life in harmony with others. The choice is yours. Will you choose life and freedom through Christ? Or the path of bondage and death the choice is yours.

The Path: We have been dealing with paths throughout this book and the Bible has numerous verses where the word path is found. I decided to include some of them to help you along your path or help direct you to the right path. I've made it somewhat easy for you. However you should go read the chapters where each one is found in order that the Holy Spirit might use them to help you find the path to freedom. Sometimes it is really not about the journey that you take but the path by which you get there. Sometimes the twists and turns of life are all because we are on the wrong path. The path to freedom is the one that you need to take in order to break the chains of bondage. Find the right path. Be encouraged and blessed and *Don't be afraid to walk in the Rain* Minister Mike.

(Numbers 22:24) But the Angel of Jehovah stood in a path of the vineyards, a wall on this side, and a wall on that side.
(Job 28:7) There is a path which no bird knows, nor has the vulture's eye caught sight of it;
(Psalms 27:11) Teach me Your way, O Jehovah, and lead me in a plain path, because of my enemies.
(Psalms 77:19) Your way is in the sea, and Your path in the great waters, and Your footsteps are not known.
(Psalms 119:35) Cause me to walk in the path of Your Commandments; for I delight in them.
(Psalms 139:3) You search my path and my lying down, and are acquainted with all my ways.

(Psalms 142:3) When my spirit fainted within me, then You knew my path. In the way in which I walked they have secretly laid a snare for me.

(Proverbs 1:15) My son, do not walk in the way with them! Keep back your foot from their path,

(Proverbs 2:9) Then you shall understand righteousness and judgment and honesty, every good path.

(Proverbs 4:14) Enter not into the path of the wicked, and go not into the way of evil.

(Proverbs 4:18) But the path of the just is as the shining light, that shines more and more to the perfect day.

(Proverbs 4:26) Ponder the path of your feet, and all your ways will be established.

(Proverbs 5:6) lest you should meditate on the path of life, her tracks are movable; you cannot know them.

(Isaiah 26:7) The way of the just is uprightness; O Upright One, weigh the path of the just.

(Isaiah 40:14) With whom did He take counsel, and who instructed Him and taught Him in the path of judgment, and taught Him knowledge, and made known the way of understanding to Him?

(Isaiah 43:16) So says Jehovah, who makes a way in the sea and a path in the mighty waters;

Closing Prayer

Father we THANK YOU first of all for the completed work of Calvary and all of the assurances that it provides us with. In this life and the life to come, we THANK YOU for the opportunity to share words of instruction, hope, and encouragement with your people. Lord please break the yokes and chains of those who are bound. Whether it be of their own doing or a time of testing. Father help them to know that you are there through your Holy Spirit and with your guidance and help the best is yet to come. Lord show them the path to freedom and help them to stay on that path. Help them to daily walk with you and continue to choose life in Jesus name we pray Amen.

Links:
My website: https://ministermike.wordpress.com/
http://www.makersdiet.com/ (while I have not tried it personally I've seen and heard a lot of positive things about it. So it may be a good starting point. Always consult God along with professional advice before starting a diet.).

Made in the USA
Columbia, SC
14 November 2024

46102679R00028